Direct Messages

C B

BookLeaf
Publishing

Presentation by *BookLeaf Publishing*

Web: www.bookleafpub.com

E-mail: info@bookleafpub.com

ISBN: 9789357440936

First edition 2023

DEDICATION

This book is dedicated to all the women who have ever felt neglected, unloved, unheard, outcasted, martyred, manipulated, isolated, or misunderstood in any life circumstance. You are not alone.

ACKNOWLEDGEMENT

I want to thank all the haters for being my motivators.

PREFACE

Writing this book was a way for me to put my feelings onto paper and explain my side of my divorce. It's been healing to process my emotions and get them onto paper creatively. I've learned on this journey that when it comes to feeling uncomfortable emotions and processing gut-wrenching life events, there's just no way out but through. These poems are direct messages for the people who never even cared to ask me my side.

White Picket Plastic Fence

From afar,
it looks the part.
Sturdy, secure.
But when you approach,
your focus becomes clearer,
and you see its truth;
mismatched pieces,
flimsy material.
You can see the frustration
that it took
to put it together,
which is so apparent
in its assembly.

Things aren't always
what they seem.

Moving On

It's bittersweet,
this goodbye.
We both know
it's the right move.
I'll never forget you
or how you changed me.

You kept us safe.
You kept us warm.
Shielded from the outside,
you embraced me on the inside.
You showed me
who I really am
and who I could become.

Witness
of soft moments
in the night,
and chaotic moments
in the day.
You witnessed it all.
You were there
for it all.

Your protection was
my safe haven.
You were the only one
I could rely on.

You were my cocoon.
This metamorphosis
took place within your heart.
But now,
I must fly...

Tears stream down my face now
happy and sad
nostalgic
grateful
reminiscent

You never failed me
You did the best you could
We have just grown apart
You'll always have a piece of my soul

You were ironic
Just enough
All I needed
The best and worst
Everything
but not enough

I was grateful
yet bitter
I need more...

Goodbye 16 Village Road

A Married Single Mom

2 babies
2 dogs
2 houses
1 woman
1 man
the latter
less than half
the time
0 support
0 unity
tons of bills
lots of chores
endless responsibilities
not enough time
to get it all done as
1 woman
not enough time
to think
not enough time
to feel
a human machine set on autopilot
to do, do, do,
go, go, go

the woman's job:
to take care of
everyone else
and everything else

the man's job:
to go to work
and
take care of the woman.

and when he doesn't...

she learns
to take care of herself

Breaking Point

"She needs a break.
I'm giving her a break,"
That's what you always told everyone;
It wasn't like that, though.
I didn't just need a break
from the constant, incessant nature
of stay-at-home-mom-hood,
always selflessly at the mercy of others,
with no breaks to decompress.
I needed a break from you.
You couldn't recognize my suffering,
you wouldn't hear me out.
You wouldn't share your own feelings on anything.
"I don't want to burden you with my problems!" you said.
My feelings are not problems,
or burdens,
nor are yours,
if you even have any.
Relationships demand communication
attention
work
listening
understanding
empathy
respect
None of these you gave back to me,
when I gave all of mine to you.
So, what I needed was a break
from your blatant neglect.

I finally had a breakthrough
that thankfully lead me to choose
to break up...

Now,
go break a leg
as you act in the show
that is your life.

The Ways of the Road

He threw her under the bus
before she even had a chance
to cross the road.
He imagined
she was out hitchhiking
for whoever would pick her up.
He was actually asleep at the wheel,
dreaming up his own reality.
She was desperately pounding
on the outside of his truck window,
yelling and begging to open up.
Being outside for so long
with cries going unheard
and causing all that commotion,
someone noticed.
A criminal saw an opportunity.
He kidnapped a vulnerable victim.
Made her feel she was safe with him,
then he shoved her out of his vehicle
without slowing down,
on the scariest
most abandoned road
there ever could've been.

Your Truth

9

the perfect husband
the amazing friend
the hard worker
the funny guy
the best dad
how dare your wife
betray you like that?
you poor thing.
such a perfect person
wronged in such a hurtful way.
she must really be
a terrible, horrible person.
who does that to someone?

A Lobsterman's Legacy

The name of a boat
is much more than just a name.
It's its reason for being.
It's telling
of the fisherman's soul,
his pride,
what motivates his work.

Does anyone know that I named yours?

Radio

turn on
tune in
hear
listen
communicate
or change the fucking station

Big D Energy

Big Disappointment
Big Dishonesty
Big Delusions
Big Downfall
Big Dumbass
Big Divorce

Your Superpower

You're right about one thing.
I am "a hateful and miserable person,"
when I am married to you.

What does that say about you
as a husband?

You have the power
to transform a
loving
giving
nurturing
smart
thoughtful
selfless
happy
funny
witty
sweet
confident woman
into the worst possible version
of herself.

Bravo.

Level Up

Lose
Everything
Very quickly and
Evolve
Lovingly

Under all the
Pressure

Simple Relationship Math

addition is including something new
subtraction is taking something away
multiplication is crashing the power of two
things together
division is splitting one thing by force of
another,
resulting in it becoming smaller.
in all four processes, there is one final product.
but the product will be different
based on which equation you choose

calculate wisely
the numbers don't lie

Emotional Property

16

If only
our emotional property
could be divided

I had my life savings invested

While yours was locked away in a trust fund

Her Truth

Only when he found dirt
did he smear her name
because otherwise,
what would he say?

She's divorcing him
because he doesn't
make her happy.

A narcissist's nightmare,
for anyone to believe
that he's not the perfect image
he portrays himself to be.

The Underdog

The person
that wasn't expected
rises to the top,
despite the adversity
that they faced
to get there.

The adversity
acting as the catalyst
that got them to that point.

Enormous strength is gained
which creates momentum
to embodying the feeling
of being absolutely unstoppable.

So who's the underdog?

Human Sacrifice

I can walk through hell's fire
and come out colder than before.

Solid as an iceberg.

You can try to burn me
but motherfucker I'm fireproof.

And I actually sink ships.

An Act of Self-Care

my "affair"
was an act of self-care.

desperate to be seen,
I clung to the first sign of having been.

empty in my soul,
I had to do something bold.

something to make me actually feel,
something that I hoped would turn out to be real.

never intending to cause harm or hurt,
just wanting to get fucked and learn how to
squirt

mental health is so important
next time I won't choose a dude that's impotent

That Good Karma

Keep
Allowing
Reality to
Manifest
Authentically

The Way Back Home

Hurled out of a moving car,
lying in a ditch
in the middle of the night.
Confused, shocked, lost.
Where am I?
What just happened?
I look around.
Nothing is familiar.
Nothing makes sense.
I'm all alone.

I have two choices.
I can lie here,
accept my fate,
and die here in this ditch
where the world thinks I belong.

Or,
I can stand up,
brush myself off,
and try to find
my way back home.

But where is home now?

If I just wander aimlessly
and never find home
anywhere in this outer world,
I've never felt more at home
than I do now
within my inner world.

Taking this messy,
unbeaten path
is certainly
my destiny.

Freedom of Speech

A police car drives by.
My 3 year old says,
"I wonder where that police car is goin'...
maybe to go get bad persons
to take them to jail."

I asked him what kinds of things
people do to have to go to jail.
"Maybe they say a bad word,
then they'll go to jail."

This is a moment
for me to teach him
about the freedom of speech.

I tell him that anyone can say
anything they want,
even bad words.
People can't go to jail
just for saying bad words.

But even a 3-year-old's logic
recognizes that you're a bad person
when you publicly slander your wife.

Your freedom with words
is spreading misinformation,
half-truths,
and controlling the narrative
of rumors in the community.
Gossiping behind my back.
Reading screenshots of messages
that you invaded my privacy to get,
after we were divorcing anyway.
And fake as fuck Facebook statuses.

How I use my free speech
is by confronting people in public
face-to-face
who blatantly try to shame me
because they think I'm below them
and can treat me with zero respect.
But I keep my head held high.
Staying quiet on social media.
Not giving a shit what the egregore is.
Then I write a fucking book
to speak my truth

That's the difference between you and me

Encore

great entertainment
doesn't end
with unresolved drama

the good guy
needs the happy ending
the bad guy
needs to get smacked with revenge

an amazing story
ropes the spectator in
with that shocking
stomach-dropping
drama
and takes them on
a rollercoaster ride
of loss
growth
evolution
happiness
freedom
change
sadness
emptiness
grief

selflessness
acceptance
contentedness
fulfillment
trust
gratitude
complete rebirth

everyone loves a good comeback moment

Drum Roll Please